The Art of
EMCEE-ING

An easy to follow step-by-step guide for the aspiring hip hop artist

by stic.man of dead prez

BOSS UP INC.
REAL RECOGNIZE REAL ®

Boss Up, Inc., P.O. Box 310330, Atlanta, Georgia 31131

The Art of Emcee-ing

ISBN: 0-9770092-0-3
LCCN: 2005928921

Production Coordinator: Stic.man for Boss Up, Inc.
Cover Photo: Shannon McCollum
Cover Concept by: Stic.man
Cover Art Design: Ithan Payne Creative
Consulting: Reginald S. Muhammad
Editing & Formatting: Abena B. Muhammad
Layout: www.convertthewack.com

Published by Boss Up, Inc.
P.O. Box 310330
Atlanta, Georgia 31131
bossupinc@comcast.net

Printed in the U.S.

ACKNOWLEDGMENTS

Thank you, thank you, thank you to my family, comrades, friends. Mama (Nora Gavin), from day one your encouragement has helped to keep me inspired and give my best in what I do.

My lady, Afya has always given me her honest opinion and feedback. Her input continues to help me develop more universal concepts and better songs.

My brother and partner-n-rhyme, M1, the other half of Dead Prez is a generous friend and loving teacher. He has given, and continues to give me, lessons in political education and everything else in between.

2 Pac, Wu-Tang Clan, Big Daddy Kane, Rakim, Ice Cube, JT Money, Ice T, Trick Daddy, Outlawz, Chill Rob G, M1, KRS-ONE, Kool G. Rap, Spice 1, Lil Wayne, DMX, Snoop Dogg, Brother J, Mobb Deep, B.G., Antoinette, Bone Thugs, Andre 3000, Goodie Mob, Boots Riley, Jeru, Onyx, Last Poets, Gil Scott, Kam, Lyte, Marcus Garvey, Black Panther Party, BLA, Malcolm X, Ludacris, Michael Jackson, Stevie Wonder, Sade, Will Smith, AZ, Boot Camp Click, Da Brat, Common, Boss, T.I., Slick Rick, Black Thought, Mos Def, Jay-Z, Nas, Martin Luther, Erykah Badu, Lauryn Hill, Whodini, Melle mel, LL Cool J, Trina, Epmd, Q-Tip, De La Soul, Large Professor, Brand Nubian, Scarface, Geto Boys, Beatnuts, B-Real, Busta Rhymes, Fat Boys, Souls of Mischief, Soujah Slim, Redman, Latifah, Jadakiss and so many more… You all are some of my greatest inspirations. Thank You.

to the emcees and song writers
of yesterday, today and tomorrow...

just tell your story....

CONTENTS

INTRODUCTION

The Art of Emceeing is the first book of its kind. This is not a book about the history of rap. Nor is this a book about who's who in the industry. This book is about the *art, science and techniques* of emceeing. It gives you a step-by-step instructional guide on learning to conceptualize, write, record, publish and profit from your own songs. You will learn how to conquer your writer's block and never be uninspired again. You will learn how to beat the industry pimps by controlling your own publishing. You will learn all this and more in *The Art of Emceeing!*

Rap music and hip hop culture became a part of my daily life through my big brother, Troy. I always admired how cool he was. He would put me up on all the new songs that he thought were hot. I had already fallen in love with soul music and I owe that to my Mama's fine taste in the Blues, Gospel and R&B. I was blessed by how she would sing around our house, sharing her voice, her feelings and always, words of wisdom. My big sister Tuwanna was into Prince, Debarge, the Commodores and groups like that, but she wasn't too keen on her lil' brother handling her records. But you know I had my ways. Thanks Sis! I fell in love with all the music around me but Hip Hop was my first calling. When I started writing raps I was about eleven years old. I would write down my favorite emcees' lyrics, line for line and change a few words to put me and my crew up in the verse. Big Daddy Kane, Rakim, L.L., Too-Short, Epmd...man, listen!

I loved to just be in front of my box on the floor all day, soaking it all up. It was the local talent shows and rap contests around my hometown that gave me the opportunity and encouragement to start writing *my own* raps. My first songs were really just some super long run-on sentences. I would just go on and on until I couldn't think of any more rhymes. My subject matter would be random. In one verse I would jump around from bragging about my "microphone skills," to spitting game at the ladies, to black life in racist America; all in one, very long verse! I was just having so much fun expressing my thoughts and my little flavor. At that time I had no idea that I would one day travel the world emceeing, making a living for myself and my family, doing what I love.

Over the years, many people and factors have helped cultivate my love and talent of emceeing. I was exposed to the performing arts theatre by two very talented, Afrikan-centered actors and poets, Babatunde Imhotep and Bro. Raphael. They both gave me loving and masterful lessons in history, lyrical content, vocal delivery and presentation on stage. One of my old school running partners, Dank, was one of the dopest emcees I had the pleasure of knowing back in the day. He shared his insight and CD collection with me and we would build for hours on end about rap style and technique, writing and free-styling and sharpening each other. Another heavy influence came from my friend and musical mentor, Robert "Rook" Rucker. He is a self-taught, brilliant Jazz drummer, composer and music teacher from Miami, Florida. He introduced me to Jazz Music and Jazz Musical Theory. He taught me about being "in the pocket" of the beat. He mentored to me about complex lyrical syncopation and how to choose a "flow" that accentuates the rhythm of a beat instead of clashing with it.

Listening to Scarface, and Bone Thugs and studying their storytelling abilities has helped to shape my understanding of plots and drive, cause and effect. When I read somewhere that Tupac was a screenplay writer, I too, began to study screenplay writing and I gained an even greater respect for his musical work. I began to see a lot of classic principles of storytelling in his work. It was a great power and command of the craft he had; a scientific brilliance and emotional commitment, all in one. With dead prez I have had the opportunity to work with, touring and learning from many great known and unknown artists. From Big Pun to Jay-Z, Mobb Deep, Larry Blackman of Cameo, The Last Poets, the Roots, Onyx, Brand Nubian, Martin Luther, Bone Thugs-n-Harmony, Common, Outkast, Public Enemy, Afeni Shakur, Organized Noise, Wu.Tang Clan, Kanye West, The Fugeez, Young Bloodz, Femi Kuti, Goodie Mob, Mos Def, Too Short, The Outlawz, David Banner, The Marley Brothers, Paris, The Coup, Killa Priest, Tragedy Khadaffi, and Erykah Badu, just to name a few.

Dead prez has been recognized by the Source magazine for Lyrics of the Year as well as Lyrics of the Month collectively and individually. Our lyrics are currently used in public and independent classrooms as teaching and discussion tools. We sincerely appreciate the opportunity to do what we do.

I put this book together to serve the community by sharing my experience and perspective. I've been a student of the art of emceeing for over nineteen years (nine years professionally with dead prez) so you can say *The Art of*

Emceeing is a collection of some of my most essential notes that I've been taking in "class."

There are so many talented brothers and sisters that just need a little tweaking here and there and they will be on their way to success. Many times managers, production companies and labels will get in naive artists' heads and try to change who they are and what they want to say. The artists can feel overwhelmed and vulnerable because they don't have the experience or understanding to be confident about what they do. But no more!

Whether you want to create, write and record a hot song or make your already great songs even better, I'm confident that *The Art of Emceeing* will be a valuable investment in your career.

It is important for me that this book is presented and taken in its proper context. Mastering the art of emceeing, in my opinion, is a lifelong process. I am an enthused student that is grateful for the opportunity to share my limited and incomplete interpretation of the basics. I have so much more to learn, and so much room to grow. In writing and doing my research for this book I have been blessed with so many new insights from other writers, just about writing itself as an art form, beyond emceeing. This has been a true blessing towards developing and strengthening my own skills of *e*ffectively *m*astering *c*ommunication, *e*xpression and *e*ntertainment. (*emcee-ing*) But enough about me.

The basic information you need is here but you are going to have to bring three things to the table in order to get the most out of this book.

You must have:
1. A willingness to believe in your own talent and develop your knowledge, awareness and skills.
2. Dedication of time, focus and concentration for writing, research and practice.
3. Openness to constructive-criticism so your songs can be the best they can be.

Be proud of yourself for taking your career seriously. You are on your way. Let no one and nothing stop you from reaching your greatest potential!

stic. man
dead prez

CHAPTER ❶
What is an Emcee?

"Power is ability to define phenomenon and make it act in a desired manner." -Huey P. Newton, Minister of Defense & Co-Founder of the Black Panther Party

A rapper is another word for emcee but it doesn't carry the same weight in credibility. Anybody can be a rapper. You just say some rhyming words to a beat and you are rapping. You can even sell millions of records rhyming to a beat. But if you want to become a successful artist all around with not only financial success but longevity in the game and respect and appreciation from your peers and the world community at large, then you're talking about being an emcee!

What is an Emcee?

An emcee is a creator, innovator, communicator, orator, translator, teacher, visionary, representative, thinker, convincer, speaker, story teller, messenger, poet, griot, a writer, master of ceremonies, historian, leader, reporter, a vocal instrument, philosopher, fan, an observer, a student, therapist, social analyst, evangelist, a minister, professor, sales person, motivator, mack, charmer, host, and artist all in one! To be an emcee means that you have respect for the art of rapping and that you are proficient in the many different aspects of the craft.

Let's look at it like this. A rapper is to an emcee what an average street fighter is to a trained martial artist. They are both fighters but the degree and depth of their skill is very different. The rapper, like the average street fighter, has a few basic skills that he has learned that have worked for him in certain situations and earned him a little respect. For example, a one shot knock out punch for the street fighter and a knack for punch-lines for the rapper. But other than having a few basic moves and a little bit of heart, the average street fighter is out of shape, he holds his breath when he's punching, he's only strong with his right hand and weak on his left, he's high all the time, he bullies people weaker than him, and he thinks he can't be beat.

Now, let's do the knowledge for the martial artist. S/he works out regularly to stay in top shape, he religiously practices proven techniques with various sparring partners to further develop his fighting skills, he practices breath control to increase his energy and endurance, he can fight with not only his hands but his feet, knees, elbows and he is also formidable with several weapons. He is trained to fight well under fatigue and multiple opponents at once. And still with all these many deadly skills, the true martial artist is humble because he has a spiritual understanding that allows him to know that he can always improve. As you can see, both the average fighter and the martial artist are in the same basic category but their level of skill is many, many degrees apart.

An emcee is a martial artist in his or her craft. Yes of course, he is a rapper but with exceptionally developed skills. He is more than just an average rapper because he is dedicated to doing the best that he can at all times. He can operate with proficiency on any beat, any subject, any style and maintain his integrity and prowess. He is a warrior against limitation of his ability and expression. He sacrifices much of his time with his friends, family, job and so forth to perfect his craft. He is not just satisfied with "whatever comes out" and though an emcee must be ever confident, he is self-critical enough to recognize and solicit feedback in his areas that need strengthening. He is outspoken, passionate and convincing. Breath control, storytelling principles, rhythm, enunciation, spontaneity and improvisation, language innovation, charisma, accountability to community principles, and trendsetting are all a part of his basic arsenal. And like the etymology of the word *kung fu*, emcee essentially means *skill*. It is a title that many can claim but the crowd that has been moved is the real verifier of that skill.

It is not my intention in this book to provoke the "back-packer" versus the "bling" type of artist argument. I think it is divisive and counterproductive. All artists should be respected for their contribution to the profession. Commercial success and artistic integrity are not mutually exclusive. Just because you are a starving artist does not mean you automatically have more skills or that you lack them. And conversely, just because you are a platinum selling artist it doesn't mean you have no integrity to the roots and artistry of hip hop. Nor does going platinum guarantee you respect or that you are beyond artistic improvement. You must understand that artistic credibility and financial success can, should and do, work together wherever possible.

There are also many people I consider great emcees who don't rap at all. Malcolm X was a great emcee because of his ability to speak on behalf of so many of our people with heart, clarity and honesty. He was a street-wise storyteller able to teach and uplift through his stories and experiences. He was a master of analogy. He could motivate with the truth from the hood to Harvard, keeping his integrity and spreading empowerment. Muhammad Ali was also a great emcee. He conquered his opponents psychologically through his improvised rhymes before he even got in the ring with them. That's emceeing. One of my good comrades, a well respected, as well as a commercially successful emcee, is Common. Here are a few jewels that he dropped on what makes an emcee.

COMMON ON EMCEE-ING:

"Man, emceeing is an art. When you pick up a mic you gifted to be able to write first of all. And it's a way that you express yourself that show that you a true emcee. Like an emcee can get on any subject matter and take it there and let the people understand, hear, enjoy and feel what he saying. An emcee is somebody that come from the heart or the imagination and make it a beautiful piece. See emcees create art. They paint pictures with words.

See an emcee also is dealing with the character of the person. An emcee can go to any situation; a wedding, a funeral, a ghetto concert where the stuff is just messed up. But he can handle it because a emcee got character too. So not only being able to write but it's about who you are as a person and how you allow that to come across as a person through your emceeing. And also, emcee-ing got to do with style; like the style that you was born with. A lot of people feel that they can learn style. You can grow within your style but you born with a certain style that you were given. God gave you a style. So you develop that style.

Man, it's important for emcees to keep they publishing because you know when you write, like if you got the rights for what you write, your words gonna be here forever. Ain't no telling when it might sell and become a goldmine, you know. So other people can't just use your stuff without your permission. You know, I can say for real, I done did a publishing deal. It's times that I heard my stuff in movies that I ain't even know they had cleared it for. So it's important if you able to and can do it at that time to keep that publishing."

Above all things in this book, we are focusing on that aspect of an emcee that empowers him or her as *a song writer*. Many aspiring rappers, poets and the like are talented in one aspect of the art but need to be more well-rounded in order to reach their full potential. This is that opportunity. Hopefully, this text will be an inspiration and a helpful tool in your success as an emcee. Maybe you will write the new, improved version in the years to come and share your insights and experience with the community. But first things first; let's get into the nitty-gritty!

CHAPTER ❷
So What U Sayin'?
No More Writer's Block!
How to Get the Ideas Going and Keep Them Flowing

"A picture is worth a thousand words." -Anonymous

This chapter is about creativity and organization. Two qualities every professional emcee must have. You are on your way to making your creativity serve you in a reliable and organized manner. After you have finished this chapter you should have a good understanding of how to always have an endless supply of ideas for your songs. There is plenty of useful information, whether you have an idea already that you want to begin with or you are stumped and need a spark. Let's assume you need a spark.

What is Writer's Block?

Writer's block is a condition in which you can't think of anything to write about or you have an idea but you don't know how or where to start with the song.

How is it Caused?

There can be a lot to deal with in our lives such as taking care of our families, hunger, fear of failure, stressing to get that paper, relationship issues, time constraints, unproductive environments, etc. Lack of exposure to new ideas and experiences can also cause a case of writer's block. Take, for instance, you have managed to write a few songs for your album but it seems like you keep saying the same thing over and over. You want to have a well-rounded album but you have seemingly run out of things you want to say. I usually get a case of writer's block before and after we complete an album so it's definitely a normal thing that happens.

How Does it Affect You?

It's very frustrating when you feel you have no inspiration. It causes an artist to miss deadlines, which means missing opportunities and, bottom-line, missing out on money. In extreme cases it can get to the point where you start to lose confidence in your ability all together. But wait... there is a solution.

How is it Solved?

What you need is a "**concept**."

A CONCEPT IS A TOPIC WITH A SPECIFIC POINT OF VIEW

First, a **topic** and a **concept** are two different things. A topic is a general subject, category or idea. It could be one single word, an old saying, a popular phrase, or any such basic statement or idea that rings a common bell for you and other people to identify with. It is extremely key to start with a good general topic because *your topic gives birth to your concept.*

Now, the concept is *not* all the details, but it is the *specific idea* that you want to expound upon in your song, *based off the topic.* Your concept is the context that holds together the music, lyrics and title. Once you understand the difference between a topic and a concept, you've got the battle with writer's block already half won. Let's use an example to make it simple to grasp.

Take for instance, *here's your topic; jail.* That's a topic. That's a subject. It's very vague and general to where you can springboard from that subject and talk about all types of specific issues related to jail in whatever direction you choose. But now, take for instance you want to talk about *how so many of your homies got court cases at the same time. Catchin' Cases, now that's your concept.* It is based on the topic of jail, but it is specific in addressing the epidemic of people getting caught up in the system, in particular. So the key is this: ***A topic is the general idea and the concept is the specific idea for your song.***

Once you are clear within yourself on what your topic is, you can focus in on your concept. When your concept is clear, that gives you an edge right off the top. As you continue to work on your songs, you will bear witness that the concept is the seed that the rest of the song grows from. Always use it as a guide for choosing the right ideas and lyrics that "fit" in the song. But how do you know what fits, you might ask?

Staying Within the Scope of Your Concept
This simply means that there are parameters of what your concept covers that you must stay within to remain on course with your song. If your concept is "catching cases" you don't

want to stray and start talking about your emcee skills or the name of your group in the middle of your verse. Be critical and train yourself to aim and direct your creativity within the scope of your concept. Many emcees are over confident because of their "love" for the mic, but have developed no real skill when it comes to communicating and sticking to a clear point. I know, as a listener, once the rapper starts wandering off in random directions so does the listener's attention. And likewise, when you do stay focused on your concept, line for line; so does the listener's attention. This is called being *effective*.

Writer's block can also strike because there are too many ideas instead of a lack of them. To solve this, you simply have to specify and stick to one idea at a time. As you learn the science of writing your verse, you will use each verse to cover its own particular angle of your concept. By establishing your concept and staying within its scope, this will help to keep your thoughts organized so they are focused and natural, not wandering, scattered and hard to follow.

Here are a few examples of concepts for songs:
Concept: *Trust Nobody, Trust No One*

This concept could be about how you feel under attack by the system, people and circumstances surrounding your life so you don't trust anybody! You could express how you are going to make your plans happen regardless of fakers and haters.

Concept: *Love Conquers All*

Love conquers all could be about how your Mama's love and sacrifice helped you or someone else grow up and survive through hard times. Or, this concept could be a story about how Jesus was a Black Revolutionary preaching the gospel of truth to the poor people and though the Roman police killed him, they couldn't kill the spirit of his message of unity, love and peace within the poor communities he ministered in.

Concept: *Power to the People*

This could be about black people receiving the reparations that the United States government and European powers owe Black, Brown, Red and oppressed people worldwide.

Concept: *Pool Party*

This could be about a summertime day when all of your homies are around and having fun at the pool. There is plenty of beauty and lots of festivities.

Getting *Your* Concept

Now, let's get you going for *your* song. Before you can actually start writing, you must know what you want to do with the song. Determine the following:

(A) Is it **your song?** If it's your project, you can refer to the Ideas List that follows below and get cracking.

(B) Is it **a collaboration** with someone for your project? If it's a collaboration determine some things that you and the other artist(s) have in common or want to say. Then refer to the following list for a creative spark as needed.

(C) Is it a **song for you to sell to someone** for them to do it? If you are going to sell it to someone, try and sit down with them if at all possible. If not, study their previous material, see what they like, notice their strengths, style, subject range, etc. Find out what they want. Something crunk? Something reflective? Something hardcore and raw? Refer to the Ideas List below as needed. Remember, in this instance, the final product is not *your* song. The artist you are writing for must relate to it as if he or she wrote it him or herself.

FIFTEEN WAYS TO GENERATE SONG CONCEPTS AND LYRICS

1. Keep a small notebook, voice recorder or a laptop. You want to develop a good habit of writing down and or recording your ideas. The ideas will be there when you need them. The bottom-line with writer's block, is letting ideas flow into your consciousness without judging them beforehand. Freestyle. Write poetry. Whatever pops up can be a link to a great idea.

2. Create a schedule and a set writing time if at all possible. Many rappers/song writers believe that they can only write "when *it* hits them." However, this is not true. The mind is infinitely creative and even when we are asleep our minds are constantly working, managing our inner workings and sending us dreams and insights. Point being is that the mind is always in creative mode. Being doubtful of that fact is one of the biggest blocks to your creativity.

Some say, "But it don't feel natural to sit at the same time, every time and write." Well, first of all, this set writing time is not the *only* time that you can write. This is only a consistent time that you have set aside to train your mind to respond when you want it to. Secondly, everything in nature operates in a scheduled and ordered manner; the seasons, the cycles of clouds and rain, the rising and setting of the sun and definitely the mind. Organization is natural. The ritual of a set writing time will allow your mind the rhythm of order that it craves. The key is to establish a routine that helps the mind feel encouraged to do what it does best. Once you have tried it for just a couple of times, you will be amazed at how in tune you can be, at will, to your creativity.

3. Use the power of an outline to your advantage. Before you start writing your lyrics make an outline (an overall sequentially organized list) that covers all of the main points you want to make in the song. When you are writing and you get stuck refer to this outline to remind yourself what it is that you ultimately want to say. If it is agreed that writer's block is defined as not knowing what you want to say, then writing an outline prior to starting your lyrics will eliminate that problem. How? Because in the outline you have already decided what you want to say.

By doing the outline first, you also eliminate the pressure of simultaneously thinking of rhyming words, how you want to flow, your story line etc. By separating *what* you want to say from *how* you want to say it, gives your mind more power to focus on each area separately, providing you with not only stronger content and more creative expression of it, but you will be able to have this skill *at will*. This is essential for the professional. You can create a general outline before you begin the song and even mini-outlines for each verse, bridge etc.

4. Make a topic list of everything you are interested in.

5. Read. Develop a healthy habit of reading on a regular basis. A good book is filled with ideas and points of view that you can draw inspiration for a song topic from.

6. Write down interesting book titles at the book store. Write a song about what you think it would be about.

7. Go to a greetings card section in the mall. They have lots of categories to choose from and many encouraging messages that can make for great inspiration for an uplifting song.

8. Practice creative visualization and meditation. Get your tablet or computer, sit in a quiet, comfortable place and environment and think of a scenario; something you saw on television, something that happened to you last week, something you dreamed about, etc. It can be real, fantasy, happy, sad, sexual, energetic or whatever your heart desires. Now that you have chosen the "mood" of the scenario, visualize the characters involved. I mean really "see" them. What are they doing? They key here is detail, detail, detail. How are they related to each other? What do they want from each other? How do they feel about each other? What are their strengths? Weaknesses? Goals? What problems are they trying to solve? Are you one of the characters? What point of view is the story unfolding in your mind? Are you watching it like a distant observer? Are you involved directly in the scenario? Continue to brainstorm, asking and answering more questions of yourself, to bring out the specific details. You will give life to many themes, and you should have a basis for a story line.

9. Build with your homies. Chop it up about life. Dig into their brains and take interest in their insights and experiences. People usually like to talk about themselves and this will give you generous amounts of unique and real life material for inspiration. Also, you can spark conversation with people at airports, welfare offices, bars, beaches, bank lines, etc.

10. Pinpoint the major theme or even an actor's line from your favorite movie and do a song from that spark.

11. Listen to some of your all time favorite songs. In one phrase or sentence write down what the song is about; its general subject, not the details. Take for instance, Sade's classic *"Nothing Can Come Between Us."* The general idea is loyalty and commitment in a relationship. *You* could write about *loyalty* to a cause, to your homies, etc. The main point is to identify the subject and reinterpret it in your own concept.

12. Get out of the house. Take a walk or a drive. Go to a park or a club. Put yourself in an environment where activities are going on and ideas will sprout from there.

13. Listen to a radio station that you don't normally listen to. Say like a Rock, Country or even a Talk radio station. There you will find a fresh source of inspiration for topics and concepts.

14. Listen to some beats and brainstorm. Write down the words, phrases, themes and scenes that you intuitively feel in the music. Review the ideas that are most common in your brainstorm. Use this theme to come up with your song topic and concept.

15. Create a working title. Pick a popular phrase and let that be your premise for a concept. See Chapter 6 for more details.

So there you have it. It's simple. Thinking conceptually is the solution to writer's block. Now, once you have your ideas flowing, you will need structure to turn your ideas into a song. But before we build your understanding of how professional songs are structured, we need to discuss how to get the right music, in the following chapter, How to Pick a Banger.

The Perfect Beat
HOW TO PICK A BANGER

"You have to be able to hear color."-Quincy Jones

Learning to Hear With Your Eyes and See With Your Ears

There are many things about the musical production of a song that the emcee/songwriter must understand to make the best finished product possible. Some artists prefer to have the beat first before they come up with a concept. Others will have a concept, idea or even lyrics first, that just need to be "put" to a beat that "fits." This chapter will be useful for whichever way you prefer. Let's start with the basics.

What is a Beat?

A beat is the music that you are doing your song to.

Where do I Get Beats?

Beats can come from samples (pieces of pre-recorded music), from original programmed sounds (drum machines and **sequencing** keyboards), live musicians or a combination of all three.

You want to become a collector of beats. The more options you have, the more versatility you can have. You can get beats to write to, from up and coming producers and professionals alike. Or, if you have access to studio equipment, you can make your own beats. If you have access to musicians, you can really get your music options cracking. Once you get some options to choose from, here are some important things to check for to make sure you are getting a *banger*.

Know the Difference Between a Beat Maker and a Producer

Beat Maker

Generally, a Beat Maker is one who programs a simple **loop** (samples or short musical phrases that just repeat over and over) and s/he shops this around to record labels, artists or producers for sale.

Producer

A producer may or may not program a loop, but the producer is the one who develops the loop into an arranged and developed song composition. S/he does this by either programming different parts of the song him/herself that aid in the expression of the songs concept, or s/he employs the talent necessary to bring that vision into being. The producer is a storyteller with sound. Even when the song concept is not a direct narrative, the producer sees a story. S/he must see a beginning, a middle, and an ending. S/he makes sure the vocals, music, lyrics, title, and concept are all in harmony in the final product.

If you have a producer by the above standards, they'll guide you along pulling out your best to fit their, and your vision. No problem. But if you are working with a *beat maker*, you as the songwriter must take on the job of the producer. Why? Because a repetitive loop does not make a song! There must be composition. There must be planned musical accompaniment that accents your vocals. The bottom line is the final product will reflect *you* and since you want a *professional* product, there must be a vision and coordination of all the musical and vocal elements to maximize their effectiveness and impact on the listener. We will be going into detail about each part of the song next, in Chapter 4, but for now we want to focus in on how to find the beat with the heat.

Which Comes First, the Beat or the Rhyme?

Personally, I like to have the beat first in order to write a tight song. Now that's definitely not always the case. Sometimes a whole rhyme will just pour out without even hardly thinking about it, but that doesn't always happen. For those of you with that gift of instant masterpieces on tap, this part of the book wouldn't be applicable to you. But for those of us who some times need an edge, I recommend writing **to** the beat for two good reasons: tempo and rhythm.

Tempo and Rhythm

Quincy Jones said, "Finding the right tempo is *key* to making a great song." Your tempo is the speed of the beat. In technical terms its how many bars go by in a minute's time. Your rhythm is the complimentary patterns of instrumentation, the groove, the pauses and the swing that keeps your head nodding in approval while you listen or dance to a beat. When you don't have the beat first, you are not writing to a known speed or pattern. This means your choice of words and your breathing needs, may not fit the beat that you end up choosing for your song. A lot of amateurs (and pros, alike) go to the studio with pre- written rhymes and then end up forcing them onto a beat that they are hearing for the first time and the result is less than their best to say the least. I have done this and come out with a weak and unprofessional product because I could have taken my time and matched the beat with a custom fit flow. When people hear the record nobody knows all that. You can't make excuses and explain it. All they say is, it's either "hot" or it is wack!

Here are some other basic things to consider when selecting your music:

Sound Quality – This refers to three basic things:

1. The noise around the music. What goes into a recording is ninety-nine percent of what you get out of it, so you don't want to have a hissy, or muffled sounding beat to start with. Avoid the idea of "fix it in the mix" at all costs. Listen for crispy yet warm. You want thumping, clear drums; rich, full and realistic keyboard sounds and instruments. Unless done so deliberately, the bass should **not** distort over the other music, nor should any one sound stand out away from the rest of the beat.

2. The skill of the programming. Do not choose any beat in which you can blatantly hear an imperfection in the repetition point where the drums or the sample loops around. That choppy loop will make your final product sound rushed and sloppy, lacking finesse.

3. Richness and clarity in each instrument. Now, you *will* have room in the mix to enhance and tweak some level of the sound quality but the worse it is going in, the harder it's going to be to fix it in the mix. If it sounds great going into the mix and you have a competent engineer, your song will really sound great coming out.

The Feel

The mood and classification of the music is a touchy part because everyone likes what they like and they have every right to. That's what makes music so great; its diversity and ability to touch anyone who can feel it. Never lose your sense of what you feel. This section really just offers assistance in helping you find out what's best for you.

Mood

Mood means what state of being or emotion does the music provoke immediately upon hearing it. This is called *seeing with the ears and hearing with the eyes.* If you don't feel anything else, make sure you can feel the *soul* in the music. How do you know what soul is? When your mind is seeing pictures, body is grooving involuntarily and your spirit is inspired by some type of emotion, you are feeling soul. Always make sure the mood of the music agrees with the concept you have chosen.

Genre (Pronounced JOHN - ruh)

This is basically a French word for the category of music in the music industry that your beat would most likely be labeled as. I don't get too caught up in all the divisions. Where I'm from, good music is good music. Don't let genre categories limit your creativity and versatility. Now with all that being said, there *are* some natural categories that help to identify with your particular audience's tastes; Hard-core, Soul, Rock, Crunk, Dance, etc. What you want to do is make sure you are in the right vein for what you feel and where you want your music to go.

Sound Elements – These are the things to look for in the beats you choose.

A range of notes played on an instrument or sung by a voice that are a part of a harmonious group is called a *scale*. Some people can intuitively hear the "right" keys or notes in the scale, but most of us need training. Any note played outside of that scale will sound *sour* to the ear. Many amateur beats have this common problem; the wrong notes at the wrong time.

You want to begin studying and appreciating harmony, chords and basic music theory so that you can identify "clashing" notes and melodies in the beat, thereby avoiding the beats all together or suggesting or implementing corrections. No, you don't have to become the next Stevie Wonder, but you should consider taking a few basic piano lessons, just to get a good foundation. Once you learn the scale concept it will help you tremendously in choosing or even creating your own beats that are "in key." Music theory is a complex course within itself but it is definitely relevant to emceeing because emceeing is a holistic craft. You have to be well-rounded musically to be as effective as possible.

Compare and contrast sounds within a beat. A beat with contrasting sounds is very interesting to the ear. A low bass sound is accented greatly with a hi-frequency piercing sound. A mellow ambient sound works well contrasted with sharp, crispy drums. Avoid a beat where the drums are muddy, the bass is muddy and the other sounds on top are muffled and dull. Also avoid a beat that has bright crispy drums with no bottom in it, bright keyboards with no bass element, etc. Look for balance in the type of sounds in the beat and make sure it is well-rounded.

Instrumentation and sound effects can be used to create unique resonances that intrigue the ear and mind. They hold the attention and capture the imagination. Look for the producers who love experimenting with rich and creative sounds, whether sampled, pre-programmed keyboard sounds or live instruments. In my experience, these producers are usually the ones with the more unique and distinctive styles and they are fun to work with.

However, "uniqueness" can become quirky and nerdy if the sounds have no contextual substance. That means you don't want to have a glass shattering sound effect in your song if you have no thematic reason in your song for glass to be shattering.

Sample issues must be worked out if you will be selling your music legally. Watch out for beat makers and producers that use the popular obvious loops and samples. Why? This is because if you will be selling your music legally, you are going to end up paying double. You have to pay the producer for the beat then you have to pay the people they sampled from, too. Some of these samples end up costing ten to twenty thousand dollars. You get stuck because you've spent all that energy and studio time to do the song, and then you get hit with another bill. Even worse, in some situations, the original song owner that the sample came from won't even grant you a license to use it! And if they do, not only are they going to charge you a fee for the sample, they are going to charge you a percentage of the publishing profits "your" song will be generating. I'm not saying there are no situations that it can be worth it. I'm just putting you on notice in order to prevent you from an expensive problem later.

Make wise decisions based off of your entire game plan and you'll be fine. Don't be afraid to go with live musicians.

That's what sampling is for the most part anyway; sampling what somebody played live. As far as "Hip Hop rules" of what is authentic, I feel like it's the skill involved in *how* you do it that makes it authentic or not. Dr. Dre, the super OG producer of legendary groups like NWA, Snoop Doggy Dogg and 50 Cent, creates music that is full of live musicians and nobody can front on his level of production quality or authenticity as a Hip Hop producer.

Originality is important. Avoid a copy-cat beat maker or producer. When your music sounds like a secondary version of someone else's trademark sound, you lose respect in the profession. Beat makers and producers are constantly trying to "get on." Many of them are innovative and original and this brings them attention, recognition and respect for having their own sound and niche. But there are always the get-rich-quick mentalities that think copying the sound of whatever is on the radio is actually being creative. Back in the earlier days of Hip Hop we had a word for this. It was called **biting!** Now, of course a beat can borrow certain trendy innovations. That's called staying up to date; having a hip sound. Be respectful of other beat makers and producer's innovations and never choose a beat from someone who blatantly steals other producers ideas and ingenuity. As an emcee you want to be known for and associated with nothing but originality, creativity and respect.

Get the homies' feedback.

Ask your homeboys, girlfriends or anybody whose opinion you respect, to comment on the music in question. See which beat moves them immediately. Which beats do they **all** like? Ask them to be specific about what they like and don't like. This is a good way to "test" the beat and get other people's reactions. It's okay to like what you like regardless of what others like, but since you want to effectively communicate through your songs, you have to be able to see what other people see as well.

CHAPTER ❹
The Blueprint
Make a Plan

"A journey of a thousand steps begins with one step."
–Sun Tzu

At the beginning of creating any song, you need to create for yourself, a simple tool called a *blueprint.*

What is a Blueprint?
A blueprint is the sequence in which the lyrics and music occur in the song, also known as your **arrangement.**

What are the Basic Sections of a Song?
The basic sections of a song are the intro, chorus, verse, bridge, vamp, outro, break, pre-chorus, and post chorus. These "sections" make up the basic building blocks of your song. All these parts must "fit" together and make sense as a whole. The order and frequency in which they occur depends on what your creativity calls for.

Laying the Foundation
A song is a piece of music that unfolds over a period of time. The smallest unit of time we will be discussing is the *bar.* *A bar is equal to four tick-tocks.* If you were to count aloud

to your beat in rhythm, 1-2-3-4 or (tick-tock-tick-tock), that would equal one bar. That first tick count is what is called the "1." The "1" in the 1-2-3-4 sequence is the beginning of the bar and it is your time marker. You can determine how many "bars" you want each section to be.

HERE IS A CHECKLIST THAT WILL HELP YOU DEVELOP YOUR LYRICS FOR THE MAIN THREE SECTIONS OF YOUR SONG.

OVERALL:

Writing the Chorus:
- Grabs the attention
- Easy to remember
- Easy to sing along
- Makes you want to repeat it
- Communicates the point of your song

Writing the Verse:
- Grabs the attention
- Sets the scenario
- Conveys details and makes your points
- Goes out strong into chorus or next segment

Writing the Bridge:
- Grabs the attention
- Expresses a new point of view in the song, or a same

point in a new way, perspective, flow, etc.

- Asks or answers a question
- Segues smoothly back into chorus or verse

Understanding the Standard Parts of a Song

Intro:

This is any sort of musical and or vocal *set up* for your song. It breaks the ice of whatever you are about to discuss. It should heighten the interest in the song's concept. It should grab your attention. It should ask a question musically that is to be solved when your beat actually officially starts. It should basically set the tone or context of your song's essential concept.

Chorus: (general)

The chorus is the main point of your song. It glues together your verses and all the other parts of your song. It is usually repeated at least three to four times in the song. It is the heart of the song. The chorus should be easy to remember after just one listen to your song.

Verse: (specific)

The verses are the veins of your song. They explain the chorus. Verses give the details that expound on the concept and the chorus. The verse is usually expressed in two to three measured sections that share the common theme of expressing the overall concept but different details and sometimes different angles. Standard lengths vary anywhere from *eight, twelve and sixteen bars.*

Bridge or Vamp:

The bridge, also known in my studio as the *vamp*, is like an extra chorus. It's a different way to say the same general point of the chorus. It could also be an alternative view point of the song. Basically a bridge breaks the monotony of the verse-chorus-verse chorus framework and adds a surprise or twist in the music, melody and lyrics of the song. It can be *four, eight, or even sixteen bars* commonly.

Outro:

The outro is the creative manner in which you end your song. It is the icing on the cake. It can be a simple fade out or it can be a lyric that you say acappella (without the beat); whatever you so desire. The basic concept of an outro is to go out as good as you came in. Mix it up. Try new things. The more ways you can innovate, the more your songs will stand out. Here are a few basic ideas:

1) Have the record scratch sound rip into an echo.
2) Have the mic feed back and simulate that you threw it down and broke it.
3) Have a fade out that goes out but comes back two or three times.

Have fun with it. you want to make that final moment

powerful enough to have the listener remember it and look forward to it when they replay the song.

The Break:

The break is when the emcee shuts up. Let the track breathe. Let the beat knock so that your audience can feel the beat by itself. As the Godfather of Soul, James Brown would say, "Let the drummer get some!" The break can be anywhere you want it, even at the beginning. A standard place to use a break is after two verses have passed. It can be any length but it is usually about four to sixteen bars.

SPECIAL TOOLS:

Pre-Chorus:

A pre-chorus is a lyrical or musical phrase that segues into the chorus that is repeated right after each verse and right before each chorus segment. It is usually no more than two to four bars.

Post-Chorus:

A post chorus is a lyrical or musical segue from the chorus back into the song that is repeated *after* every chorus.

So, there it is. We can sum it all up like this. A blueprint is the plan of how your song sections are sequenced. It's great to be able to write good freestyle lyrics but using a blueprint will help you build well composed songs.

CHAPTER ❺
Lyrics
Painting Pictures

"Be like water my friend." -Bruce Lee

What are Lyrics?

Lyrics are the words, dialogue and "scenes" of your song. You have to instantly grab the listener's attention. An emcee/ songwriter has to be able to communicate what he wants to say in the least amount of time using the most vivid and descriptive words. Writing a song is not writing a book. Get to and stick to the point and make every word count.

Types of Lyricists

Some rappers write for the sake of word play. Let's call them the *Word Players*. Their lyrics are flooded with rapid displays of words and syllables. Now vocabulary is good because it allows for vivid clarity when used appropriately. The use of multi-syllable words requires a good level of puzzle solving skills because of the complexity and rarity in finding matching, rhyming words. The downside to this, however, is after you listen to their songs a few times you start to realize they aren't talking about too much of anything in particular, they are just rambling with a flashy show of words. Many times they have too many syllables in their choice of words which comes off sloppy and off beat.

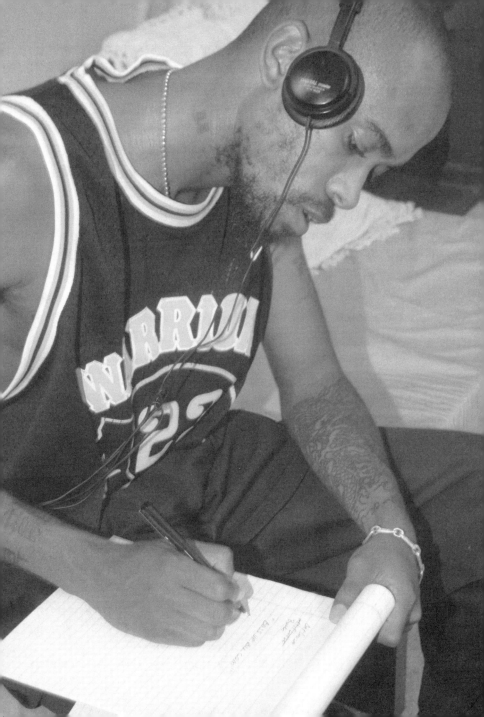

On the other hand, some rappers write in styles that are extremely simple. The *"I ain't no rapper" rappers*. No frills, no figgedy-figgedy; just line after line of straight forward raps. This is also good, because it is easy to follow and understand, but the downside is that they tend to focus on *what* they are saying far more than *how* it is being said. This can often lead to a boring and monotonous flow that lacks any kind of rhythmical sophistication.

Another common style of rapper is the the *Alter-Ego Character*. This is that extra hyper, wild and crazy rapper that becomes his alter-ego character on the mic. His rap is really more yelling and screaming than anything else. Although this is a great expression of originality, confidence, passion, vocal control and endurance, this can easily become annoying, uneasy to understand and even corny.

Still another type of rapper is the *Lecturer*. This rapper is well read and versed in many subjects like history, spirituality, etc. There are facts and truth bursting from every line of his flow. This is a great style of rap because it teaches and shares important information. The downside comes when the rapper gets so self-righteous and preachy that the audience is alienated and feels talked down to.

What you want to have is a healthy balance of *all* of these elements – a skillful and appropriate use of rhythm and vocabulary; an easy to understand delivery; a passionate, unique and original expression; and lastly, the awareness and sensibility of how to include useful content that can feed your audience knowledge, motivation or inspiration in a commonly relatable way.

Be confident in your talent but also be humble. No one is a master of everything but we can master certain things and keep improving in others. Don't assume whatever you do is automatically hot and gas yourself up. Stay away from *yes* men. Ask for and be open to honest, objective feedback. You don't have to be something you are not, just don't limit yourself in what you can be. Be your own motivation and encouragement as well as your own worst critic and you will be able to give your best effort in all that you do. The more that you practice your strengths and acknowledge and work on improving your skills where you need to, the more you will see new doors of opportunity and success opening up. Guaranteed!

Seeing with Your Ears

Before we actually get started writing let me introduce you to an idea that I call *finding the natural subject*. This is a spiritual belief I share with many emcees and songwriters in that music has an inherent destiny and purpose that you are helping it to fulfill. For me, this is where I meditate to the music and let it "tell" me what subject and concept I can help it to express. When you first listen to a beat, there will be all kind of random thoughts. Out of these random thoughts you will start to see a theme that is consistent. No matter how diverse your thoughts, the majority of them will start to be related to each other, indicating to you what the natural subject is. You want to develop your intuitive sensibilities to hear what the beat is asking for. Don't force lyrics and concepts on a beat. There are of course, many possible expressions that a song can take form in. However, in a given setting there is usually that "one" that speaks to the essence of the music and your spirit, that tells you in your gut and in your heart, "That's it." Then you are ready to write.

Your Audience

When writing your lyrics, you have to always consider and anticipate your listener's perspective of what you are saying. You are not just rapping to hear yourself rap or stroke your own ego. As an emcee you are a voice of the voiceless. Your rhyme represents what many people go through or feel but don't have the words to express themselves. You are speaking to the truth and experience of your audience as well as yourself. Appreciate this. A rapper likes to hear himself rap just for the sake of rapping and s/he's satisfied with that, but an emcee strives to communicate (strike a common chord) with the listener. You got to come *from the heart* to connect to your listener's heart.

Content and Substance

Content and substance refers to what are you talking about overall in your song. It's the significance in the real world of the points you are making in your lyrics. Since you have been made hip to what a song concept is in the writer's block chapter earlier, your lyrics should have no problems conveying the substance of your concept. Either from your own experience, research, imagination or someone else's is where you draw upon for your details. You want to know that what you are saying is true and accurate so if you are in doubt or you are not drawing upon your own experiences, do your homework to get real facts.

Content Must Stick to the Concept

As mentioned in Chapter Two on writer's block, the content in your lyrics must stay within your concept and not wander to random subjects. Anybody can ramble on and on, but an emcee is a communicator and can control his skill in a way that can focus and express a clear idea without wandering off. A wandering plot in lyrics reflects the wandering and un-centered state of the mind that created it. Control of thought is not only part of mastering emceeing but of self. Making a good outline is one of the best methods I know of how to keep your concept and content in alignment.

Starting an Easy Outline

Whether it be novels, magazine articles, business documents, movie scripts or etc, all professional writing is developed through a process of brainstorming, research and structuring (outlining). This allows for organized and effective communication of your idea and conveys it in a complete yet concise manner. In other words, it ensures that you don't forget anything that you want to include; it reminds you where to put what and it keeps you from putting in random and unnecessary information. Here's how an outline is created.

Write your idea down like this:

1. MY IDEA
Write your song concept down in a <u>complete</u> sentence.

2. THE BRAINSTORM
List any and every related thought, word, phrase, scenario, skit, sound, etc that comes into your mind. Be open about it and whatever comes don't judge it, just write it down.

3. THE OUTLINE
The outline is your pre-song arrangement guide and it helps you to think in *song* mode instead of *rap* mode. In the chapter on blueprinting, we discussed how you can arrange and re-arrange the order of which part goes where, but at this point just fill in each part with whatever ideas you have.

Intro:
Chorus:
Verse 1:
Verse 2:
Verse 3:
Bridge:
Outro:
Miscellaneous:

To illustrate the ease and functional practicality of creating an outline let's do an example. Check it.

1. MY IDEA:
   Pool party; celebrating the summertime at a pool party!

2. BRAINSTORM
   Bikinis
   Swimming
   Music
   Bar-B-Que
   Water games
   Sunshine
   Family
   Children
   Dating
   Drinks
   Water
   Splash sound effects

   Now, you can decide the best consecutive order to express your points. Build to a climax, then resolve. Once you have identified what natural order they should appear in the song, write them down as categories like in the following example of how your "Pool Party" outline would actually look.

3. THE OUTLINE
   Intro: splash sound effects, children voices playing
   Chorus: talk about sunshine, girls in bikinis, friendships and celebrating

Verse 1: describe scene...chlorine, bar-b-que grilling, feeling good, schools out, off work, what you are wearing, name your friends, etc.

Verse 2: beautiful girl appears, she likes you (or, if you're a female, vice-versa), y'all are playing pool games and flirting

Verse 3: somebody who deserves it gets pushed in the pool for fun, food on the grill is ready, everyone is having a ball, you and pretty girl take food "to go"

Bridge: love for the summer, hotness, coolness of water, the refreshing satisfaction of a year-long anticipation of summer

Outro: radio announcer voice talking about the great weather and the perfect day for a dip in the pool, sound effects of happy people, children playing, splashing, etc

You can also even draw pictures that help you remember the intensity level of how you want to deliver certain parts of your lyrics if you are not using a tape recorder at that moment.

Now that you know what you want to say and how you want it to unfold you can concentrate on the lyrical flow that you need.

Building the Right Flow

What is flow? You hear rappers talk about how *nice* their *flow* is. You hear compliments like "Son's flow is tight!" But what does that really mean? A *flow* is two things. One, it is your technique for emceeing. It's whatever style of delivery you are skillful at; your trademark style. That is one definition of "flow." The other definition of flow, which is the more scientifically useful one for our purpose here, is "the ***metered*** pattern that carries the words you choose for your lyrics." In other words, your flow is the *rhythm* that your lyrics follow and express. It can change for each song, each verse or even each line.

Crafting a good flow is a lot like doing a puzzle. In a rap lyric the syllables, pauses, pronunciation, wit, energy of your performance and tempo, all determine the parameters of what is a "good" flow or not. You will have to be creative and have a wide variety of vocabulary options to come up with the right word with the right meaning. Oftentimes you will be writing a lyric and you will be stumped and can't seem to find a certain rhyming word to answer your previous line. You will have to know how many syllables will fit in the space you want and therefore you must learn to count syllables in words. Additionally, you must rehearse and gain proficiency in the following areas: staying on beat (timing), clarity of speech (pronunciation) and clarity of ideas (articulation).

As long as you are consciously controlling your flow, staying on beat, and clear in your delivery you're good. The problem arises when your flow is sounding jumbled, stiff or sloppy and going rhythmically in places that you don't want or need it to go because of your lack of understanding how to control it. That's where this next section can help you.

Timing

The most basic skill of all the elements you need is rhythm; the ability to rap in sync with the beat. Other necessary skills are controlling your breathing and emphasis during your delivery. Timing is commonly called "being in the pocket." When I first began to take my career in emceeing seriously, I would listen to artists like Big Daddy Kane to study timing. I would copy down his entire verse word for word, memorize it and practice saying it. Doing this, I would notice the breathing requirements, the pauses at certain words and phrases and the parts that were particularly harder to pronounce and deliver. So I rehearsed hour after hour consciously being experimental with when to inhale and exhale. I had to realize that some words that you say are not fully pronounced in order to stay on rhythm. You say enough of it to imply the word but give yourself that extra split second to continue on with the delivery and stay on beat. Kane had mastery of his flow so once I could mimic his cadence and enunciation, breathing when he breathed and emphasizing what he emphasized, I started to grasp the idea of timing. I admired his skill and professionalism and I began to insist on perfect timing in my own delivery. You can listen to CDs from break beat drummers or Jazz , Latin or Afrikan drumming and study the high hats, the different layers and multi-rhythms of percussion, to give you inspiration for creative flows to use. Yes, you can copy the "flow" of a high hat or percussive rhythm to pattern your lyrics after. The possibilities are endless once you get the hang of it. Give it a try!

Syllables

Just in case you are not familiar with what a syllable is, let me break it down. It's super simple! A syllable is the slight pauses or sections in the pronunciation of a word between vowels. Take for instance the word "publishing." (1)Pub- (2)li-(3)shing. Pub-li-shing has three syllables. The word "good" has only one syllable. The phrase "caught-in-the-game" is a four syllable phrase and so on. Being aware of how many syllables are in a word or phrase is the key to writing to a set pattern and flow.

Freestyling to Find the Flow

While listening to the beat, I like to use a freestyling technique that I call **scatting** to help me pre-plan the right flow that I want to use. Scatting is basically using made up words (multi-syllable sounds with no meaning) improvised to a beat to determine the particular pattern of lyrical cadence that best rides the beat and allows you the most balanced control of pronunciation, timing and other key factors.

It's really a lot simpler than it sounds reading it. All you do is just start freestyling whatever *feel* that you want to express and start paying attention to the pattern. Use your recorder to log many different takes. You can scat or freestyle. You can try an older verse from another song. You can even try lyrics from your favorite rappers song because again, you are focusing only on the pattern and *how* it sounds not *what* you are saying. This scatting technique is very helpful because once you scat the right feel for **how** you want your lyrics to feel and ride on the beat, you then have a custom made pattern to follow. Now you can begin to go back and "fill-in" the real words that express *what* you actually want your flow to say.

Wit

Wit is subtlety and cleverness in how you use words and their meanings. Wit is the tactic in which you choose to say something. Being witty means you are resourceful in creating cool, catchy and clever ways to phrase and express your ideas and lyrics. The art of developing wit is about having a sense of humor and irony. Wit is about bending and blending words and their usage. It's about double meanings and implied but not spoken statements. Wit is being innovative and original in use of slang and catchy terminology. The lack of wit is reflected by a boring set of dry lyrics with no real flavor or spirit about them.

Pronunciation

Speaking your words articulately and clearly is to an emcee what hitting the target is to a sniper. The better your ability to pronounce your word choice with ease and finesse the more accurately your lyrics can hit your audience. When you speak in a jumbled slur to flow in a style that you haven't mastered the mechanics of, you appear to be very amateur. Practice words and phrases that are hard to pronounce relentlessly and if you can't master its pronunciation after many practices, change the lyric to something that you can say well. Now, remember, don't get so anal about it that you start to sound all-proper and corny. The point is to not be lazy or sloppy with your practice and to be sensible in your word choices to what you can fluently say. Your vocals and lyrics should flow like a natural conversation. My check and balance is pretty much "if I can't say a certain word or phrase without fumbling then don't say it, find something else!"

Point of View

The point of view is the perspective that you are telling your song from. Before you can start writing your actual lyrics you need to be clear in your own mind what point of view you are going to approach them from. Here are ways to approach expressing your lyrics:

- From you - like a personal testimony -- I, me
- From you and someone or others --- we, us
- From your observation --- he, she, it, they, them

Decide the point of view that is the best vehicle to express your concept and **stay consistent** throughout each segment of use in the song.

Past, present or future? A Tip on Tense

Tense is the time period your song is happening in; the past, present or future. There is nothing hard about it. Just decide, stay aware of and stick to the time period in your lyrics so your song makes sense.

Types of Rhymes

The whole idea of rhyming is that at different points in your lyrics, certain words or phrases correspond that sound alike. In other words, it's call and response. Whatever you start with must be answered, back and forth throughout the verse. You can invent any pattern that fits what you're trying to do.

Standard Rhymes

Rhyming words that have the same exact ending sound are called **exact rhymes**. They are words like *guerilla* and *tequila* or like *Malcolm X* and *album text.*

Innovative Rhymes

Of course all lyrics don't have to be exact rhymes. There are what I call **innovative rhymes** like *hustler* and *culture*, *radar* and *sugar*, *warrior* and *worrier* or *social* and *hopeful*. They sound very similar but they are not exact.

Non-Rhymes

Then you have the unorthodox. These words are related in context but they do not rhyme at all like *automatic* and *automobile*, *understand* and *under the gun*, etc. It could be any combination where you deliberately lead the listener into "expecting" a certain word but you use a non-rhyming word instead. This adds the unexpected to your flow and breaks up the monotony of every line being a predictable flow. Use these with reservation because a song with too many non-rhymes becomes poetry or just plain speaking.

Rhyme Patterns

The A-B pattern
The most common and basic pattern for rap lyrics is the A-B Pattern. It is expressed like this: A=B (Line A rhymes with line B.) Here's an example:
"The police want to **lock me up**, (A)
but I'm way too smart for them to **box me up**." (B)

Combos
Groups of words within a line or phrases that rhyme with each other are called **combos**. An example of this would be:
"The govern**ment** at**tempts** to **pimp** us all."
From taxes to **rent,** our backs are a**gainst** the wall."

Lyrical Techniques

Alliteration
Alliteration (a-litter-ation) is a big word for using words that start with the same letter. It's the age old "**p**eter **p**iper **p**icked a **p**ickled **p**epper" type of thing. Tupac (RIP) used this technique very well on his song "If I Die Tonight." **S**ee if you can **s**eason up **s**ome of your **s**ongs with the **s**ame beginning **s**ounds in your words like I have **s**o **s**adly done in this 'S' **s**oaked **s**entence you are **s**oaking up now. **S**mile!

Verbal Sound effects

The Wu-tang Clan, especially Chef Raekwon and the late Old Dirty (RIP), brought a whole lot of lyrical innovations to the game. One of their credits was the clever use of verbal sound effects. The "click-click! blow! blow!" gun shot sound written and delivered verbally was so original and creative. It not only caught our attention but it did what good lyrics are supposed to do, show you better than tell you. The legendary emcee from New Orleans, B.G. has innovated one of the most popularly used terms in the game to date: Bling-Bling! I know that that phrase is way overused and has come to even represent, to many people, the capitalist aspirations of the rap game, but you've got to give credit where credit is due. B.G. is a master lyricist when it comes to his storytelling and innovative slang style flow. He could have said my chain is shiny. He could have said his jewelry glows. But no, he let the chain and jewelry speak for themselves. "This is what my jewelry is saying when I walk in the room, Bling-Bling!" Verbal sound effects can enhance the marketability of your lyrics tremendously when used sparingly and in proper context with your song. Experiment and be original!

The Overused Simile and the Overworked Metaphor

"My rhymes are like spoiled hot sauce. They got sick flavor!" "I rocked so many mics they call me the meteor man!" You have undoubtedly heard corny rhymes like this before. What these terrible examples are attempting to use as a lyrical device is the comparison technique of simile and metaphor. Whenever you use "like a…" or "hard as a…" you are using a simile. When you make a reference in comparison to something like (rocks) *rock*ing so many mics to a meteor shower (thousands of rocks falling in the sky) you are using a metaphor. I've heard too many rappers kick verses where every single line is "like a this" and "like a that." To me, that is called abusing the technique. It can be a great way to be clever if you use it sparingly and in proper context.

The Alphabet Tool

Here's an easy way to help jog your ideas when you are writing your lyrics and you are stumped for rhyming words. Get a sheet of paper and write out each letter of the alphabet in a vertical column (up and down). Now, just for example, let's say you are looking for words that rhyme with "bandana." You can't think of anything off the top of your head that fits in the context that you need it. This is where using your Alphabet Tool becomes helpful. You can go letter for letter and sound out the ending of bandana or anything that sounds close until you come across the perfect word you are looking for. It would go something like this.

"Bandana"

A- antennae
B- banana, banner
C- Commander, Copa Cabana, channel

D- dinner
E-Emma, enamel
F-flannel
G-grand canyon
H-handle, hammer
I-intimate candle, I don't believe in Santa
P-phantom
S- scandal
and so on...

The Alphabet Tool is great for brainstorming and thinking outside the box. You will have more options in front of you without having to use that memory space because you wrote them all down. There is also computer software you can get that has rhyming and song set-up tools to help you. "Master Writer" is a pretty cool songwriting program if you are into writing on your computer. Save and file your Alphabet Tool lists after you use them because you can reuse them again and again.

4 BASIC TYPES OF LYRICAL CADENCE STYLES

Many of these styles and artist examples overlap and they should. I present the classes here only for you to get an idea for your options. Remember, you always have the option to create a brand new style, too.

The Chant

This style carries a proud, warrior energy as it probably goes back to the Zulu chants and other great Warrior Clans of Afrika. It is enthusiastic, easy to say and catchy. The chant is great for choruses and gives your lyric an instant head nod! Lil John of The East Side Boyz is a great example of the chant. Project Pat is also a brother that represents the Chant flow very well.

The Syncopated Bounce

This style is characterized by its fast rhythm and precision. Bone Thugs and Twista, among others, have made this style popular. This style requires a great skill in coordination of breath and timing but when done articulately it is a hypnotic, fast paced flow of feeling and imagery that captivates and entertains the listener. When you have something of substance to express and you can express it in this masterful style you will cover a lot of ground in the "respected skills" department. Again, I stress that your rhythm must be impeccable to avoid coming off as sloppy.

Straight Forward

The name of this style speaks for itself; direct lyrics, line for line. No extra fancy rhythmical tricks, just solid, relatable content and easy to understand delivery. Scarface and Tupac are masterful examples of the straight forward style. From Melle Mel and KRS-ONE circa Boogie Down Productions' era, to Too-short, Jay-z and Ice Cube, the straight forward style has been a powerful tool of some of the greatest emcees of all times.

There is nothing really that technical about this style. You just say what's in your heart like you were having a conversation with your listener. It's about feeling and content more than anything else. Snoop Dogg is a great example of how a straightforward style isn't limited to being monotone and serious. He has shown the world that a straightforward style can be entertaining, funny, charismatic, clever and full of flavor and soul.

The Rubik's Cube

Like the mentally entertaining colorful novelty toy of the same name, the Rubik's Cube style is the flow that entertains the mind for the love of the craft itself. This flow is all about spontaneous rhythmical patterns of rhyme. This is what we used to call freestyle back in the day. Not freestyle in the sense that it is all previously unwritten off the top of the emcee's head but freestyle in the Jazz sense, meaning there is not a pre-set or predictable pattern of flow. The emcee appears to bring you with them through an audio cinema graphic ride that only the emcee himself knows where it is *rhythmically* headed. It keeps your attention bringing you here then there all in a controlled yet unorthodox manner. It is best exemplified in talented emcees like Nas, Black Thought of the Roots, Common, Kurupt, Lauryn Hill and others.

More on Flow and Cadence

Flow can be learned the same way that a dance routine can be learned. What you need is knowledge of the steps and lots of practice. You have to master when to pause and when to move, or in the case of lyrics, when to speak and when to breathe. This essentially is cadence. Lyrical cadence is the manner in which the words are rhythmically articulated to ride the beat.

One of the best ways I know to explain cadence is to bring your attention to the hi-hat – the bright ticking sound that keeps the beat steady like a metronome. Well in a way, this is what your lyrical flow and cadence is doing. You want to have a flexible flow but one that stays in the pocket of the swing of the beat.

The two most important things are staying on rhythm and being crystal clear in your delivery. One of the most common traits of a "wack" rapper is sloppy delivery. Words come out unclear, rushed and jumbled. In my opinion, it is better to have a simple clear flow than to spit out a whole bunch of words sounding like you have food in your mouth. Be disciplined in your choice of words. It's not just the words you say but the spaces you leave silent that creates your cadence. Pay attention to the subtle nuances in the amount of time it takes to say individual words. Notice how a word that begins with a vowel (A, E, I, O, U) takes more breathe (and slightly more time) than words that start with consonants. Practice pronunciation of the harder to say parts. Rehearse it over and over until you have memorized the words, pauses and breaths and you can perform it, at will, precisely and smoothly.

Leave Room for Breathing

Proper breathing is of utmost importance in mastering your flow. My rule is, if you can't perform a verse all the way through without running out of breath, you have to make changes in your lyrics until you can. You must learn to use spaces and pauses to silently catch your breath during your flow. Never let your listener actually hear you breathe unless it is intentional for a creative effect.

You should be able to perform your verse like you were having a conversation even if your delivery is super amped up. How is that possible? It's possible because of the spaces that you have mindfully placed when choosing your words and cadence. Let your breathing needs be a guide for where you take your flow. Don't just think of the words you want to say. That's how raps get written that are too jumbled for a beat and make the rapper's voice weaken and sound as if s/he was straining. When you have been considerate of your need to breathe at certain intervals of your flow and proactively included time for those breathes, your performance will increase dramatically!

This also translates well in live performances because you've made it easier on your voice in the creative stage before you hit the performance stage! You should learn to be mindful of your breathing in general. Many times you can be holding your breath and not even be conscious of it. Holding your breath will result in tension somewhere in your body. At any point that you realize that you are holding your breath unintentionally, just stop and take a few slow, deep belly breathes. Shake out your limbs and relax your neck and shoulders. The more you practice slow, steady and controlled breathing you will notice that you are developing a stronger lung capacity which of course contributes to enhancing what you can do in the booth and on stage.

Word Quality

Word quality means choosing vivid and descriptive words; words that show us what's going on rather than just telling us what is happening. Don't be afraid of vocabulary. It gives you choices. Just don't start sounding like an encyclopedia in all your raps. Listen to Malcolm X's classic speeches. Listen to Tupac. They are perfect examples of eloquent, yet down to earth and conversational, vocabulary usage.

Again, the main thing you want to understand is not to just use words that **tell** your audience something. You want to use words and phrases that **show** the audience what you are talking about. Here's an example.

Telling
"... I ate two helpings of food and got full."

Showing
".. After two helpings I was stuck in a trance. Couldn't even lift my fork, stomach busting out my pants!"

The telling example above simply states the facts. However, the showing example presents the facts in a way that interacts with the listener's mind and has them "see" what you mean! When you tell somebody something, they hear your words but when you emcee they must mentally "see" what you are saying.

Use of Slang

Slang is the coded expression of Black and Brown language that conveys our unique creativity, spontaneity, common sentiment and rebelliousness. Slang is dialect. It is the local words or phrases that, though commonly understood by a certain small number of people, are not generally or widely known to a larger population. Slang is words and phrases that are innovated locally and comprehension of their meanings are limited to those local users.

Here's an example in how one word can have many meanings: The word *yard* in slang terms has several meanings. To *go to yard* is to go to Jamaica. If someone sells you something that *cost you a yard* that means you paid one hundred dollars. Still another meaning is how an O.G. might warn a young person about the protocol and dangers that await you if you ever have to *spend time on the yard*, of course referring to prison life.

Hip hop has come from the language of the people and it is these common forms of expression that give Hip Hop much of its appeal and character. Though Hip hop has played a major role in popularizing certain slang words and phrases, local slang in one area may still mean the total opposite in another. In some instances, it's like foreign language from one coast to the next. So how then do you incorporate slang in your rhymes so that a vast range of listeners will understand even if they are hearing the slang term for the first time?

The key factor is context. All you have to do is ask yourself, "Can people understand what I mean by a slang term based on the way I am using it? Does the way I use the slang term lend itself to interpretation? Can someone reasonably *imply* my meaning based on how it is used in my lyric?

For example, let's use the word "*icy.*" Icy is something to describe the road during the winter months, right? Wrong! Gucci Main and Young Geezy out of Atlanta, Georgia scored a hood classic with their single "So Icy." We know what the chorus use of the word "icy" means because the brothers illustrate it in their verses; in context. They talk about having things, being financially successful and displaying that wealth and success with symbols of jewelry, expensive cars and other items of grandeur. We automatically *infer* as a listening audience that "icy" means "wealth and success." All you have to do is make sure you support any local slang term that you are using with enough information to where the average person in your target audience can put "two and two" together and understand what you mean. It's that simple. Now can somebody tell me what "Whoomp! There it is!" means? Just kidding! Let's move forward!

Rehearsal and Memory Techniques

After you write the basic body of the verse that you are satisfied with, be able to say the verse at least ten times, without reading it. This goal is to ensure your memory of your material and to expose any little imperfections in the words, rhythm or breaths that need to be adjusted or changed. By memorizing your verse before you pay for studio time you will not only demonstrate your professionalism but you will be saving time and money because you already know your material.

ADDITIONAL QUESTIONS TO ENSURE THAT YOUR LYRICS ARE SHARP

1. Can the average person sum up your overall point after one listen?

If not, you may be wandering on too many different ideas that don't seem to be related in one central way. If you can't summarize what you are talking about in one *complete* sentence, neither can your audience. You will need to condense your ideas into one theme and rewrite your lyrics so your song can stick in your listener's mind.

2. Is every line necessary or are some of them just fillers?

Don't settle. Every line you write should be significant to your whole song. When you have lines that are kind of just there to hold space and not really adding to the description, information or entertainment value of your song, leave them out. Putting in irrelevant lyrics bores your audience and causes your listener's attention to wander off.

3. Are all my words pronounced with finesse and clarity? Do I need to change some words or patterns that are sounding sloppy or off-beat?

We thoroughly discussed the importance of articulation and rhythm to a good flow. Don't get attached to something just because you wrote it. Accept nothing but your best from yourself and that's what you will get every time.

4. Are my ad-libs out of sync and jumbled? (Ad-libs are discussed in detail next in Chapter Six.)

Go back and fix them. Underline the words you want to say if you have to. Again, it's not about how quick you can finish but how good you can finish.

5. Is there any main point missing?

Keep referring to and checking off on your initial outline.

6. Did I put enough emotion into my delivery?

Consider how you want your lyrics to feel in your delivery and make sure that you get that as an end product. If the song calls for "crunk" energy don't be sounding all shy on the mic. If the song calls for a smooth and romantic feel don't yell and scream. Stay focused!

CHAPTER ⑥
Jump in the Booth
The Recording Process

"The fight is won long before you step in the ring in the training hall." -Muhammad Ali

A REMINDER ON MEMORY

One of the common issues that I have run into a lot when artists are in the studio to lay down their vocals is that they don't remember their lyrics. Brothers get in front of the mic with a piece of paper, and attempt to "read-rap" their vocals coming off sloppy and stiff. My golden principle is to be able to perform the lyric at least ten times without the paper *before* you even step in the recording booth. Don't just mumble the lyrics to yourself under your breath. When rehearsing practice performing your lyrics in the way you want them to come across. If you practice correctly you will learn correctly and therefore perform correctly. Not only will this improve your delivery one hundred and ten percent but it will save you money because you won't be wasting studio time doing a thousand takes over and over to get it right.

If you have access to free studio time, you can record a rough draft "rap-read" recording of your lyrics just for reference. This will let you hear your lyrics and their flow with out the pressure of getting the performance perfectly right. Then you can tweak them later on your own to get ready for your real performance.

VOICE PREPARATION

Warming your voice up before you record is necessary to help your vocal chords get ready to work. Your vocal chords and lungs are actually muscles. Just like your biceps and quadriceps need to be stretched and warmed up before you lift weights or take a run, all muscles need to be warmed up before working them to avoid damage and to increase their performance potential. Always remember that as an emcee your voice and your lungs are essential to your craft and your livelihood. Take care of your lungs and your vocal chords and they will help take care of you.

Three Warm-Up Exercises You Can Do Before You Start

1. Slow and controlled deep breathing for a few minutes.
2. Softly perform your lyrics several times.
3. Sing the vowels of the alphabet (A,E,I,O,U) several times.

VOICE HEALTH

I encourage you to learn as much about your respiratory system as you can. You should be aware that smoking not only eventually leads to cancer and death but it contributes to a host of other lung and throat related health problems like influenza, bronchitis, strept throat and even the common cold. Here are some holistic methods to nourish your voice on a regular basis, not just in the studio.

1. Get rest. Too many up-all-nighters will compromise your immune system and make you more likely to catch a cold.
2. Eat more veggies and whole grains. These will lubricate the membranes in your throat and lungs and provide necessary nutrients that will keep them strong.
3. Gargle with sea salt. It will sweep your throat of bad bacteria and congestion.

Here are a few more examples of "voice supporting" foods and nutritious sources.

Foods:
Brown rice
Steamed and boiled green, yellow and orange vegetables
Raw or juiced cucumbers
Miso and other seaweed soup
Carrots
Fresh lemon juice diluted with water
Strawberries
Lemon
Honey
Garlic

Herbs (ingested as tea):
Marshmallow Root
Slippery Elm
Sea Moss
Licorice Root
Marigold (Also known as Calendula)

Additional gargling options:
Warm water + Goldenseal and Myrrh (herbs)
Warm water + lemon and honey
Warm water + Sage (herb), cayenne pepper and honey

Other Items:
Vitamin C
Bee Propolis (Protects mucous membranes of the mouth and throat)
Zinc Lozenges (Immune boost)

When your voice is in distress avoid:
Cold drinks
Spices
Alcohol
Smoking

The Toothbrush Connection

The toothbrush obviously plays a major role in keeping your mouth and lungs healthy but it also can contribute to spreading unwanted bacteria because even after you rinse your toothbrush off, a lot of bacteria can still be present. To counteract this, when you are finished brushing your teeth, you can leave your toothbrush soaking in either grapefruit seed extract or a hydrogen peroxide solution. Also, every time that you are sick you should throw your toothbrush away and get a new one so that you don't reintroduce the same germs back into your mouth.

THE RECORDING PROCESS:

Quick recording tip!

Record all your final vocals in one session if at all possible because it is hard to come back on a different day and match your same vibe with vocals you already laid down. You have to milk the vibe in the moment.

Mics

Good choices of mics make all the difference in the world. You will have to test different mics out in different studios to find the best ones for your voice type and aesthetic goals for each project you are working on. At Warrior Studios, we use the U-87 and the Akg a lot. Ask the studio engineer and take notes on the different mics you come across in different studio sessions. A good way to remember the sound of your voice on different mics is to write the mic model name on the CD that has your recording on it. Good vocal mics can cost anywhere from one hundred bucks to thousands of dollars. Don't skimp on quality because it really does make a difference.

Recording Techniques

Always use a windscreen when laying down your vocals. This eliminates a lot of the "popping" sounds for words that start with the letter P. All professional studios and even most amateur studios will automatically have this for you, but if they don't, you should bring your own. You can get a decent one for twelve to twenty dollars.

You want to stand about six to twelve inches from the windscreen and point your mouth directly at the microphone head. The louder you project your voice, the more you must adjust and step back from the mic so you don't distort by being too loud and too close to the mic. You can nod to the groove while you perform your lyrics, but be mindful not to move your head around from left to right too much, because your vocals will sound like they are fading up and down when you play them back.

VOCAL TERMINOLOGY

Lead Vocal

The lead vocal is *usually* the first vocal track you start with, but it is essentially the dominant, loudest vocal track in the mix. It sets the main tone and character of your vocal delivery. Don't get into the habit of laying down a sloppy lead vocal and thinking, "I'll fix it in the mix." Lay down a solid, quality performance, correct all the errors by re-recording and then move on to your next tracks. You can try and hide mistakes and imperfections by adding other vocals to camouflage it, but the quality will suffer and you might end up wasting a lot of time trying to "fix" something you could have just gotten right the first time. My mama always told me, lazy people work the hardest.

Adding more than one vocal track in a given section of your song is called making an *ad-lib* track. Ad-libs are usually lower in volume than the lead vocal. They emphasize or add character to the lead vocal track. There are many ways to ad-lib your vocals. Here are a few.

Types of Ad-Libs

Stack – exact complete copy of the lead vocal. Good for panning. Good for chant or anthem style songs. Adds body and fullness. Great for chorus section.

 Accent – certain words and phrases are copied but not the entire verse. Great for verses.

 Harmony – lead vocal track is copied or accented in different vocal keys. Good for blending with the melodic structure of the beat, helps express passion or smoothing out the impact of the lead.

Whisper – lightly copies the lead and creates a glowing hall effect around lead vocal. Good for sexy effect. Helps pull the listener's ear into the song.

 Echo – this is an accent ad-lib that repeats a particular word in a 1/4 note rhythm to vocally imitate a delay effect.

Animation – several tracks used where character drastically changes on each track, such as George Clinton vocals creates a space-aged type feel, good for bugged out type of concepts.

How Many Stacks is Too Many?

If you sound like a group of people saying your verse you have too many ad-libs. Ad-lib stacks should be *felt* more than heard. They are for enhancing the articulation of your lyrics but never should they just be a set routine thing you do the same way every time. Your stacks should be as unique as the musical and lyrical style called for in each song. For a chorus, usually about four to eight stacks will suffice. More than that and the lyrics start to phase out and lose their clarity.

MIXING AND MASTERING

Learn More About the Basic Principles and Options

Mixing and mastering is the process by which you and your engineer edit each individual sound and vocal into a sonically-refined and balanced final recording. This final version is where all your future duplications will come from. Going into the intricate details of mixing and mastering is beyond the scope of this basic introduction to emceeing but I strongly recommend that you take the time to ask your engineer to explain it in some basic terms to you. Furthering your understanding of mixing and mastering will offer you valuable techniques to bring the proper delivery feel and articulation to your vocals after they are recorded. You will also need to ask your mastering engineer for different versions of your song. One of those versions is called a TV track and is used for your live performances. We will be discussing the TV track and more in Chapter 8 entitled Move the Crowd. For further study on mixing and mastering, check the suggested reading list in the back of this book.

CHAPTER 7

What's in a Name?

Choosing a Title for Your Song

"A name that rings bells, sells." -Anonymous

A title for a song is not just some words you take from your chorus and throw on your CD label with no thought. Yes a title should express the concept of your song, but it's got to do more than that. A title is a *marketing tool*. What you choose to call your song must speak to your target audience in a way that they can relate to and be excited and intrigued to hear it. You want to think in terms of creating a campaign, something that pulls in a lot of interest and has a life of its own; a word or phrase that can spark a conversation or set a new trend. In essence, with the hundreds of thousands of songs that exist at any given moment, your title has to stand out and get noticed.

Now that doesn't mean that your title can't be subtle or simply stated. And that doesn't mean you have to fabricate a lot of unnecessary meaning behind a simplistic concept. What it means is you have to authentically summarize your song into a title that is creative and intriguing and one that creates multiple options and avenues for your marketing advantage. Here are some basic points that can help you in choosing a great title for your song.

- The main purpose of a title is to intrigue your target listener and make him or her identify with its message.
- A title should entertain the mind.
- A title should be in the language of your audience.
- It should be easy to remember.
- A title should grab attention.
- A title should express the character and sentiment of your song.
- It should be catchy.
- A title should inspire some type of emotional response.

Create a place in your tablet or laptop for random titles that come to you from time to time. They may work for a future song or give you inspiration for a new concept.

When to Choose the Title

You can think of your title before you start writing and let that guide your concept and song development or you can write the song first then choose the title. I like to come up with a "temporary" title for while I'm writing and then when I'm done if it sticks I keep it. If I think of something better after I'm finished writing, I'll change it then.

TYPES OF TITLES

To make this section real simple let's imagine your song is finished and it's about *being successful despite the struggle and the haters*. Here are some ways you could choose a good title:

Popular Phrases, Sayings or Slang Words
"Grind til I Ball," "Bossin' Up"

Alliterations
(when the words in the title all start with the same letter)
"Paper and Power," "Live the Life You Love," "Big Bankin'"

Hook Titles
(when the title is the main phrase in your chorus)

Rhyming
"*Steady* Bout My *Fetty*"

Slogan
"Got To Get It" or "Doin' it Big"

Twist on a Popular Phrase
"*Millionaire* Man March"

Humorous
"Paid Like Oprah Them"

Add a Sub-Title to your song when the point of the song or the appeal of the title needs further expounding or when trying to reach two or more distinct audience types.
"*From Roaches to Rolls Royces*" (A tale of Rags to Riches)

Abstract
"The Color Green" (as in money; growth)

The Abstract Title

The title is the main point of your song usually summarized in about one to five words but there isn't any real set limit if you have something really fresh and creative.

You can create new slang or create a clever new twist on an old saying. Stevie Wonder uses the abstract title very often by choosing a title that is not obvious in the song lyrics at all; *Sir Duke, As,* and many more. This is a creative way to add depth and mystique and sophistication to your song if that is your goal and it fits the style you want to project. Just be mindful that it could confuse some of your listeners. Because the title is not readily apparent in the chorus when a person goes to buy your song after they heard it somewhere they may not know what to ask for, causing you to miss those sales. Feel me?

A Word on "Profanity"

Avoid using so-called profanity if you want radio airplay. To be honest, I think the whole idea that there are certain "illegal" words is a slap in the face to freedom of speech. I mean who created and then outlawed these "evil" words in the first place? I think people should use their own moral judgment for what they have to say, and let the next person express their own ideas how they see fit as well. But you know that is not how things are set-up are they? The powers that be (the infamous FCC) use "curse words" in your title or your lyrics as an excuse not to even consider your work for airtime. Of course, like any bureaucracy, they have double standards. They let certain record companies' artists say one thing and won't let other's say the same thing. The program directors are hypocrites to their own policies, projecting a superficial sense of morality judgment over the artist's right to freedom of expression. But, with all that being true, they still will front on you if you use so-called profanity, so recognize what you are up against and move wisely.

CHAPTER ❽
Move the Crowd

Stage Performance:
From Rehearsal to Sound Check, to Ready to Rock!

"To me, emcee means move the crowd." -Rakim

Once you have completed your songs you need to get ready to take them to the stage! Here are the basics of what you need to consider.

How Do I Get a Show?

You can get a show by hiring a manager, a booking agency or you can throw your own event with your friends.

What Will I Need?

You will need a few basic things to get you going. Here they are.

The TV Track

A TV track is your song without your lead vocals on it. Your chorus and ad-libs are on it. That gives your voice support on stage and helps your performance have that steady professional sound that is on the record. You request this version of your song during the end of your mixing session.

An Instant Replay Machine

An instant replay machine is about the size of a turn table. It's a hard disk recorder that you "load" your audio into. You or your DJ can program it to play your TV track songs on cue in whatever order you want. It can be set for an automatic run or it can be started and stopped manually so that you can be spontaneous with your show. The instant replay machine sounds great but one down fall is it doesn't have an internal volume control. This means you have to have an additional DJ mixer hooked up to it to control the volume levels coming out. It retails for about two thousand dollars, but it is worth it after you see its reliability in your show. You know how the CD or the record can and will skip some times? Well, not the Instant Replay machine! You and twenty other people can jump up and down on the stage all around it and still it doesn't skip! All in all, it's the best machine that I've worked with as far as sound quality and non-skipping reliability.

Now, let's move on to the keys to a great show. First up, you guessed it, rehearsal!

REHEARSAL

Don't skip this. This is where you go over the sequence and live presentation of your songs. This is where you go over the cues of your show. You'll want to have with you a DJ of some sort with the TV Track versions of your songs on wax, CD or instant replay machine to hold your music down for you. You should design and rehearse your performance a minimum of three to ten times before each show.

MEMORY

All lyrics and song arrangements must be second-nature. You must be familiar and comfortable with song order, pauses and segues.

VOCAL ENDURANCE

Make sure your vocal endurance is adequate enough to withstand a full length performance. Use this time to increase the nutritional nourishment of your voice and don't practice your full delivery the day before your show.

PUTTING IT ALL TOGETHER

You want to put together a show that is a pleasing presentation. Nobody wants to stand around and watch an emcee just stand there and rap. You have to be inventive. Be creative. Involve your audience. You have to bring them into your world and keep them interested. Use color, sound, clothing, humor, shock, popular instrumentals, smoke, moving images projected on a screen, flashing lights, dancers, acting and whatever else you can communicate effectively with. At a minimum, you will need:

- an intriguing intro
- a well balanced song sequence
- segues to spontaneously address the crowd
- breaks for your audience's attention span and for you to catch your breath
- an exciting outro

Your Intro on Stage: Captivate Their Attention

How you come on stage will be your first impression. You want people to feel your charisma and the energy in your spirit. This will enable them to relate to you instantly. Be as creative as the size of the stage and your budget will allow. Involve the crowd with something they want to see, something they want to hear. Compel them to say something they want to say and have them do something they want to do and you have their undivided attention. Use lights, music, whatever. Keep your "intro" down to about a couple of minutes.

Song Order

Come in with the heat. Get the crowd going. As your show progresses on, start mixing up the flavor. Change the tempo. Change the feel. Reveal your versatility. Then close with a solid banger.

Segues and Intermissions

Keep it short and sweet. When you stop the music you are stopping the flow of the show. However, there are breaks needed. You want to address the crowd and introduce yourself in some way and you don't want to compete with a loud beat when you do it. Now if you have a song that does that, even better, but if not make sure the audience knows who you are. You also need breaks in your show to assess the mood of the crowd and to take in feedback. You don't want to just run through a whole show with no contingency plan for the crowd's response. Make these pre-planned segues seem natural and spontaneous by not trying to say a prepared speech. Just make a general plan for each break like at the first break introduce yourself and your team. At the second break ask what hoods are present and go into a group chant on a locally popular beat. Things like that. Be original.

Your Outro: Go Out With a Bang

Save one of your strongest and most captivating songs for last so that the audience will leave feeling thoroughly satisfied and captivated by your performance. Be sure to thank everyone for coming and for their support and energy. Thank and mention the organizers of the event. Make sure people know your name and where they can get your product. Make sure you let the people know how to contact you for bookings.

Now that you've practiced and practiced and gotten your act together, let's talk about how to take it all to the stage!

SOUND CHECK

Before you get on stage in front of a crowd of people, you want to do what is called a *sound check*. This is where you and the sound engineer, also known as the sound man, do a test run through your performance. This is usually the day of the show, a couple of hours before show time where you set up and make sure all the equipment is functioning properly.

Make sure that you can hear yourself and that the music is acoustically balanced on stage. You can coordinate with the lighting engineer as well. You will familiarize yourself with the stage and make little adjustments in your show cues to accommodate space issues and crowd involvement.

If you skip your sound check, you run the risk of sounding like garbage in front of everyone at the actual show. So don't skip it. Everyone who has ever been to one knows how bad amateur rap show sound systems can be and many so-called professional ones. Even though this is a club-owner-promoter-sound engineer-responsibility, ultimately it makes the artist look bad. Insist on the best you can get out of the situation at all times. There will be bad sound for sure, but you can still have a great performance if you are pro-active at your sound check!

THE PERFORMANCE

When you know your material, you have skillfully designed and rehearsed your songs in sequence and you have completed your sound check, you are ready to rock!

Here are a few tips for your performance:

BE YOURSELF AND HAVE FUN. Remember to enjoy your performance. People can feel your energy and if you are having fun they'll have fun too. You prepared for this, now enjoy it and shine!

DON'T CUP THE MIC. Keep your fist from covering the head of the mic. This makes you sound muffled.

DON'T YELL AND SCREAM. Pay attention to how you sound in the moment; don't be oblivious. Stay aware and recognize when you are distorting or sounding muffled or incoherent and adjust your delivery accordingly. Ask the crowd if they can hear you okay, if you aren't sure. They'll let you know and you can adapt.

IF YOU HAVE A PARTNER OR PARTNERS, DON'T OVERLAP EACH OTHER BY TALKING AT THE SAME TIME. Learn each other's rhythms, be courteous to everyone's shine time and pre-plan so that everyone's input is heard and not jumbled and cluttered fighting for space.

WORK THE WHOLE STAGE. Make eye contact with the people. Address the left, right, middle, in the back, front and center, up top, by the bar – everybody.

BE HUMBLE. Arrogance will create boos. You are not the king without a kingdom. Always remember that the people must elect their greats. Always assess the pros and cons of your performance so the next one will be better. If it's not your goal, you don't have to be the greatest stage performer who ever did it. You just have to be confident being you to the fullest but always seeking feedback and ways to improve.

WHAT IF THEY BOO? Maintain your cool. Don't get all mad and lose it in front of the audience. Just keep doing your best. Sometimes tough crowds have to warm up to you. However, if you feel like the crowd *really* would like for you to get off stage, do so. They'll at least respect your maturity and then later you can reflect on how to improve your show without regretting busting somebody's head open. Feel me? But if you have been on point throughout the process of developing your emcee craft you will be able to respond even in a bad situation like booing, poor sound acoustics or what have you and still get the crowd to feel you and respond to you positively.

GET ON, DO YOUR THING AND GET OFF. Don't fall blindly in love with the spotlight. A show that went too long could have been great but it overdid it. Be respectful of your agreed upon stage time and the other performers in the event. Remember, it's not how long you are on the stage, it's how good you are and knowing when to get off. You would rather have the crowd yell out for more than for them to boo you off the stage or walk out because they are tired of you.

GIVE BOOKINGS AND CONTACT INFORMATION. In your outro make sure to let the people know your name and how and where to get your material. Be sure to announce your contact information for shows in the future and any other projects you are working on.

CHAPTER ⑨
Get This Money
Artist Rights, Resources and Responsibilities

"Don't let nobody punk you out yo' grip."
-Goldie Loc/Eastsidaz

Don't sell out! Your publishing, that is! Start your own company. It's easy and simple. Not only will you be making money, but you can write off all "company" related expenses (paper, pens, laptops, studio sessions, blank CDS, plane tickets, lunches, stamps, etc) in turn, saving money on your taxes. This chapter will break down the basics, now that you are ready to turn your songs into a money making career.

COPYRIGHT
You are the creator and therefore the owner of your work. When people want to play or use your creation in any way, they have to have your permission. Your permission is called a **license**. If they don't have your permission, they are violating your rights. You should register all your works with the U.S. Copyright Agency (until we have our own) so in theory you will be "legally" protected if someone tries to use your work without your consent.

Once you have at least one song in the market or in production for a commercial release, you are eligible to join a **Performance Rights Organization** that will help you stay on top of this process. There are fees involved in joining, but they are relatively low. You'll choose your company name, fill out a few forms and you are on your way to receiving your royalty payments!

WHAT IS A ROYALTY?

Royalties are fees (money) that you are paid as the owner of your copyright for use of your songs. There are three main ways that you get paid in royalties. They are performance royalties, mechanical royalties and synchronization royalties.

Performance Royalties

There are well known Performance Rights Organizations, like BMI and ASCAP, that on your behalf as a member, license your material to music users who wish to utilize your music live or broadcasted in the public. That means radio stations, television shows, hotels, clubs, wherever. These organizations are supposed to shop your songs around to movie producers for scores and soundtracks, video game music directors, advertising companies, etc. They are employed to secure your song's placement and financial compensation in all the international arenas that music is used.

Your royalty compensation will be tracked internationally, calculated based on how often your song is used or played and paid to you about every four months once you become a member of one of these organizations.

Do your research and choose which one of these organizations you feel can best help you make money from your songs. Again, I strongly recommend that you don't sell or give the Performance Rights Organizations, the record label, your manager or anyone a controlling share of your publishing. When you own your publishing, down the road, through the ups and down of the business, those checks add up and come in handy. If you sell it off right away for a few thousand dollars, and later you have a big hit, you might really wish you hadn't!

Mechanical Royalties

Performance Rights Organizations (the BMIs and ASCAPs, etc.) pay you your performance royalties, but *the record label must pay you your mechanical royalties*. The copyright laws in the U.S. essentially say that if you own the copyright of a song or a musical work, you have the right to profit from its *mechanical* reproduction. **That means for each CD, tape, record, dub, etc. that the record label gets manufactured and distributed, whether ultimately sold or not, you are entitled to compensation.** This is in addition to your performance royalties. The law states that you are to be paid for "all copies manufactured and distributed." The law says you are entitled to one hundred percent of the statutory rate (check with your lawyer for exact calculations of the present going rate). Record labels always try to get away with paying you seventy-five percent or less of your mechanical royalty payments due so make sure your lawyer is on point. They give it to you in what they call your advance but you have to pay that back. It's really a dirty hustle game that these labels run on the artists. Be ever focused on your business so you don't fall for the okie-doke!

One mechanical rights organization that will follow up and help you handle this process is the AMRA (American Mechanical Rights Agency, Inc.) among others. They may even audit labels if need be, or take their filthy butts to court to get your money. If you are already a signed artist with music that has been commercially released, be sure to follow through. You don't want to miss out on money you have just sitting, waiting on you.

Synchronization Royalties and Licenses

Television, video and film usage of your songs can turn out to be big paper if you are on top of your game. The rate for these licenses is always negotiable. Consider the length of use, the presence and impact of how it is placed, along with the territories that it will be distributed in to help you determine your proper compensation.

PERFORMANCE RIGHTS ORGANIZATIONS
VERSUS ROYALTY *ADMINISTRATION* COMPANIES

You should realize something about the big performance rights companies. They have thousands and thousands of artists and songwriters on their roster. They have super multi-platinum artists that are their main breadwinners. If you happen not to be one of those super multi-platinum artists you are **not** priority. You will have to keep them on point because they will not be aggressively trying to track every little local broadcast and what not that you are on. They will miss a lot of your songs because of how the big time tracking systems are set up; the little guy doesn't even register on their radar. Those unauthorized plays here and there, around the world, add up and they would have you missing out on money if you aren't aware of another way to track and get paid. Now, you don't want to sell your publishing but tracking your own radio spins worldwide and processing the paperwork for your licenses might be a bit much for you to do all by your self. You are probably going to need some help *administering* it. This is where making a partnership with a Royalty Administration company can come in handy.

There are many small staffed but well equipped independent and international companies that can pick up the slack. For a small fee of something like ten percent they will aggressively track and procure monies that you are due. They will also shop your material to artists, producers, record labels, movie soundtrack directors and video game houses on your behalf. They do not have any ownership of your copyright.

They take the ten percent off the top of the money they collect and you get ninety percent; simple, just like that. And because they are a smaller company you are more of a priority. They don't eat, if you don't get songs placed, so they are generally very aggressive and successful in getting your songs licensed in the market.

Dead Prez has enjoyed a great relationship with a company called The Royalty Network out of New York, since we got hip to them. They always pay on time, they send us quarterly newsletters that let us know who in the industry is looking for material and they even have helped secure our work on video games, films and soundtracks. I don't often recommend particular companies in the industry because the whole game is so cut throat and shady, but I can honestly say The Royalty Network has definitely been reliable and productive for Dead Prez.

My partner M-1 is a member and a spokesperson for The Grassroots Artist Movement called GAME. He has been working for several years with many other dedicated young folks to fight for artist rights within the music industry similar to how unions work on trade jobs. They have established health care options for some of their members and they provide education on the music industry and other resources to help empower the artist. You can reach out to GAME at www.kickgame.com. Stay creative, stay focused and stay up. See you on the grind!

Glossary of Selected Terms
Here are a few terms that are helpful to know.

Arrangement – The blueprint for how all the parts of a song complement each other in a sequential order.

Bar – A unit of musical time that equals the first four counts of a beat.

Dub – A duplication or copy of a song.

Emcee – A person who practices and demonstrates the art of rapping in a proficient and skillful manner. Used loosely, any great singer, song writer, orator or communicator demonstrating a great talent for verbal communication.

Free styling – The art of rhyming off the top of one's head; improving spontaneously.

Genre – A French word referring to the categorization of a song by its general sound qualities identifying its assumed primary audience base.

Key – A note in a musical scale.

In the pocket – A phrase that expresses the idea of a sound or vocal performance being rhythmically and precisely synchronized with the beat.

Master – The original final copy of a professionally mixed song.

Publisher – The legal owner of a written composition.

Rhythm – Having rhythm is the ability to hear and complement a pattern of music, keeping in sync with the beat.

Tempo – The speed of a beat. Commonly referred to as BPM, it refers to how many Beats Per Minute go by in a song.

Time signature – The amount of beats per bar. The most common time signature in Hip Hop Music is four beats per bar and is written 4/4.

Track – The digital or analog space in which a single vocal layer, instrument or sound is recorded so that it can be manipulated and adjusted individually without changing any other vocal or instrumental sound.

About The Author

The author, Khnum Muata Ibomu (Stic.man), has been emceeing for over nineteen years. He has been recognized by the Source Magazine for both lyrics of the month and lyrics of the year. He is currently a producer and one of two emcees from the internationally respected, politically active rap group, Dead Prez. They have toured and performed with many great artists such as Mos Def, The Roots, Common and Erykah Badu and have sold hundreds of thousands of albums worldwide. Stic.man is also the president of Boss Up, Inc., an independent multi-media lifestyle company dedicated to empowering the community with revolutionary inspiration, entertainment and education.

Stic.man is available for collaborations, music production and song writing projects. He can be contacted via e-mail at bossupinc@comcast.net.

Suggested Resources

1. The Science of Breath
   By Yogi Ramacharaka
2. The Wu-Tang Manual
   By The Rza
3. Q The Autobiography of Quincy Jones
4. *Blow! Magazine*
5. Atlanta Musick Bizness
   By Professor Griff of Public Enemy
   Available at www.hdqtrz.com
6. The Autobiography of Malcolm X
   As told to Alex Haley
7. Muhammad Ali's Greatest Fights: Cassius Clay vs. The United States of America
   By Howard L. Bingham and Max Wallace
8. Rhythm and Business: The Political Economy of Black Music
   Edited by Norman Kelley
9. Music, Money and Success: The Insider's Guide to Making Money in the Music Industry
   By Todd Brabec and Jeffrey Brabec

Notes

Notes

Notes

Notes

Notes

BOSS UP INC.
REAL RECOGNIZE REAL ®

To order additional copies of this book go to
WWW.BOSSUP**BU**.COM or mail a Money Order in the amount of
$24.95 plus $3.00 shipping and handling for each book to:

Boss Up, Inc., P.O. Box 310330, Atlanta, GA 31131
(Please make Money Order <u>Payable to Boss Up, Inc.</u>)

BOSS UP, INC. ORDER FORM
(photocopy or cut out & include with order)

Name

Street Address

City, State, Zip

Daytime Phone / E-mail

PRODUCT	QUANTITY		PRICE EACH	TOTAL
The Art of Emcee-ing	_____	(X)	$24.95	$_____
(+) add $3.00 shipping & handling for **each** book				$_____
Total Amount Enclosed				$_____